AF411975

Inconstant History

Inconstant History

Poems and Translations

Gregory McNamee

Foreword by Sam Hamill

Broken Moon Press • Seattle

Some of these poems and translations first appeared in
*America, The Bloomsbury Review, The Canyon
Country Zephyr, The Classical Outlook, Earth First!,
Exquisite Corpse, The Midnight Lamp,
The Wallace Stevens Journal,* and *Willow Springs.*

Printed in the United States of America.

ISBN 0-913089-15-X
Library of Congress Catalog Card Number: 90-83691

Cover photograph by Ken Sánchez.
Used by permission of the artist.

Broken Moon Press
Post Office Box 24585
Seattle, Washington 98124-0585 USA

for Melissa

Contents

Versions

Alvaro de Campos

Gonzalo Rojas

Antonio Marimón

Octavio Paz

Homero Aridjis

Foreword

ROBERT DUNCAN waited fifteen years between publication of his *Bending the Bow* and his final, two-volume *Ground Work*. He declared his intention to wait those years at the time *Bending the Bow* was published. Reviewing *Ground Work* at about the time of Duncan's death, *Publishers Weekly* declared, "Some people think he's a pompous windbag," demonstrating to what abysmal depths public opinion has sunk—even in the world of publishing—when it comes to the life of the intellectual imagination. Erudition is out; homey homilies and little poems with punch lines are in. The classics are out; nostalgia is in. Mythopoeia is out; the "self" in the form of the first-person pronoun is in.

Fortunately, there are poets for whom Modernism means more than a postgraduate seminar, for whom the classics are very much alive. Gregory McNamee's poems and translations return us to fertile ground where Sappho and Akhmatova, Octavio Paz and Martial become contemporary. His own poems are imbued with the same slightly sardonic, slightly formal spirit.

In his essay "Towards an Open Universe" Duncan writes, "The Christian Hippolytus accuses Heraclitus of teaching 'that the created world becomes maker and creator of itself.' The Greek word for 'created' being *poieitos* and for 'creator' *poieiteis*, the created world is a poem and the creator a poet."

Many of our poets have turned away from that older order, turned rather to a poetry of self-realization, excluding the mythology and history and social agitation that have been constants in poetry at least since the

Greek Anthology and the *Shih Ching*. "Our consciousness," Duncan says, "and the poem as a supreme effort of consciousness, comes in a dancing organization between personal and cosmic identity." This often-neglected identity, given voice, brings jeers from *Publishers Weekly* and the Illiterati. Pompous? Shall we have no more room in our poetry for Sappho or Martial or Tu Fu? Are the attitudes of the ancient poets and the songs they made no longer of use to us?

Gregory McNamee's poems tell us almost nothing of his personal life beyond the life of the intellect and imagination. There are no poems of domestic bliss or domestic hell; no poems looking nostalgically back at ordinary youth, now suddenly slipping away; no poems showboating the author's sensitivity. In short, there is no poetry of self-realization in these pages. But there is, of course, self-realization itself, as expressed in the making of each poem and as unified in a single book. It is astonishing to find in a first book of poems a voice equally at home with the mythical character Coyote and with Akhmatova, a voice comfortably evoking Tiananmen Square and the great delta blues belter Robert Johnson, Pancho Villa and the Days of Rage, all within one short poem. McNamee is also witty in ways very much out of fashion: "And we will lean against our broken fences / To wait for nights of endless snow, / Make plans to leave, but never go." There, in "torrents of dust," the speaker becomes an everyman, a Beckettian figure in a decidedly rural landscape.

Making poems both formally and informally, McNamee handles each with dexterity. He may be the first poet since Robinson Jeffers who can, without self-consciousness of any kind, address a poem "To the Fallen Republic" or to Yeats's Ireland without sounding like a . . . well, a pompous windbag. But perhaps most welcome of all, his poems overflow with historical resonance, with figures fully fleshed. In his poems there is a real feel for being alive within history.

He gives us versions of poems by the great and under-appreciated Mexican poet Homero Aridjis, a poem by Henri Michaux, Sappho's great "Hymn to Aphrodite," and other sacraments from various cultures, including some delicious imitations of Martial. *Inconstant History* is a formal dinner with great companionship.

To mix metaphors, I would say it is a concert, one sustained piece with parts for several voices. The arrangement is effective. In my listening over several performances I learned some things: I went to my library several times to track down players and their repertoire, only to return again for McNamee's slightly caustic humor and slightly sinister good will. There are moments when, in his formality and conviction, he sounds almost like Thomas McGrath:

> A rose in Jericho, but time ends,
> and the earth plants its sweet flowers
> in the boneyards of the Americas,
> in the ribcages of conquistadores.

Or is that music an echo of Ezra Pound? In any case, it's an ear best enjoyed in large portions, the way one turns not to a poem by Denise Levertov, but to a book; the way one enjoys reading "in" Rexroth's longer poems, in Wordsworth, in Pound's *Cantos*, or in Robert Duncan. Gregory McNamee's resourcefulness is exhilarating.

When Cleanth Brooks denounced "the heresy of paraphrase," he was simply demonstrating that poetry is more experience than meaning. Aristotle prized

more highly than any other literary quality the power
to find similarities between apparent opposites. The
"meaning" of the poem lies somewhere within the
resonance between languages, somewhere beyond the
simple language on the page, so that the poem consists
of a frame of perception made by words, the true "ex-
perience" of the poem being beyond words themselves.
Brooks believed metaphor to be untranslatable. In the
Modernist vein, however, implicit meaning takes pre-
cedence over explicit meaning. Therefore, one may
attempt to reveal—as Aristotle would—analogy by lis-
tening for resonances between cultures and languages
without violating the original.

Too few of our poets, it seems to me, have learned
the importance of getting inside the skin of another
culture, of learning to think like a Heraclitus, of think-
ing the "dangerous" thoughts of Sappho and Dante, of
the Romantics and Modernist exiles, ideas that are a
perpetual challenge to established order. Perhaps our
contemporaries, like ourselves, are just a bit too com-
fortable, a bit too complacent, to really feel the evoca-
tions of a Sappho, the happy cynicism of a Martial.
McNamee reminds us that we do not live in a blissful
bubble of consumer dreams. His poems do not indulge
the social lie. They are wrought in hard-earned intelli-
gence. They include rather than reject our history and
consequently embrace our present more knowledge-
ably, more passionately.

If McNamee is not yet as skilled in cadence as Dun-
can, if he remains for the moment too much centered
in the mind at the expense of the body, he is nonethe-
less a poet with a vision and a world and a voice. It is
not, I think, an accident that the body becomes more
imperative in poetics with advancing age—thus we

might account for Rexroth's great erotic poetry near the end of his life, or for Duncan's music centering itself in the "dance of [the] physical body" over the last twenty or thirty years of his writing. Who would be foolish enough to predict what McNamee might make in another fifteen or twenty years?

For the present, it is gratifying to hold McNamee's first sacrament, to cradle his poems in the body of the breath, and to enter his world with its many presences, its shadows and echoes and rhymes. And I think of Catullus remaking poems from the Greek of Callimachus in order to become—Catullus; I think of Rexroth's incorporation of classical Japanese poems within his own longer poems; I think of Pound's great impersonation of Sextus Propertius. I hope Gregory McNamee will continue to bring us poems and translations beautifully woven into single fabrics like *Inconstant History*. In "Callimachus at Pharos" he writes, "But I have no more songs, / and I can make no more vows to ghosts." And I know he is writing a persona, that he is only wearing the mask of Callimachus. Otherwise, these lines would be lies. Because there will be more songs and more ghosts, more masks and more vows. There is a dance between the personal and cosmic identity. Because McNamee is a poet.

Sam Hamill

Inconstant History

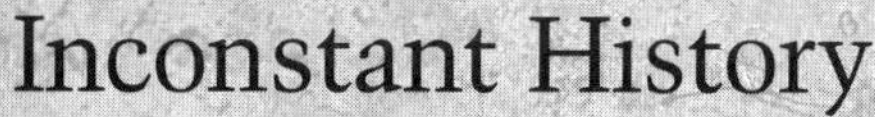

The uproar of mankind is intolerable
and sleep is no longer possible
by reason of the babel.
The Epic of Gilgamesh

Sarasvati in the New World

Solipsistic, blinking, wander
trembling, mindless, through whitewashed archways
and jade curves of chacmools,
among hyacinth, turquoise, birds of paradise,
amid the annihilating fire,
the obliterated past. Envision
Haida, Menomenee, Cashinahua, Tukano,
Kayapo, Cakchiquel, Bororo, Tillamook,
Modoc, Wampanoag, Gê, Chiricahua,
Vizcaina and Tuatha dé Danann.
Try to locate the history
that has been disappeared.
Every one of us is a foreigner now.

In the New World a new millennium
arises to erase what has come before it.
Two thousand nails in a splintered cross,
minus ten and counting, two thousand
brads carved of jade, and a rose far away
in Jericho. Who among us may gather it?
See the rose spread in Casasola's faces,
in the mummified newborns of Guanajuato,
in the murdered plowmen of Salvador,
in the open eyes of *los desaparecidos*,
in the supple noise of mountain water,
in new leather, flour cakes, raw diesel,
and dooryards full of fighting cocks
clawing at petals.
Who truly believes he has mastered these?
What, generals, is left to be commanded?

A rose in Jericho, but time ends,
and the earth plants its sweet flowers
in the boneyards of the Americas,
in the ribcages of conquistadores.
Take the black glass from its heart.
Spin it northward to dying seas,
spin it southward to dying forests,
the wounded houses of infinity.
Spin it over countless nations.
Spin it until it melts into gold.

Two thousand nails, and Sarasvati trembles
within the mouth of all eternity,
within the eyes of mythless continents.
She sings an air from the Río de la Plata
of dancing mothers and screaming jets.
She shapes a bit of bone from Chile.
She smoothes a pyramid of emeralds
and zacuan feathers, endlessly.

A cataract of new blood thunders
from red-tiled rooftops everywhere.
A hundred million flowers wither.
Sarasvati, mother of all we will never see,
Athena, mother of our emptiness,
Nuestra Señora, blessed trinity,
none among us can know why you ever smiled.
Foreigners, we walk between gates of flame.
Where now are the ears to hear our prayers?
Who can live within a wall of fire?

A Theory of History

No birds woke up
When Anthropos died.
No widow cried.
No one spoke up.

But the next morning snow
Lay as always on the ground.
An old man and a crow
Built Anthropos a mound.

And Anthropos shivered, cold
In his grave.
He froze where he lay
In the black earth's fold.

A laurel is blooming
Over Anthropos's head.
And the birds have just noticed
That Anthropos is dead.

Instructions to Aries

Illuminate
no path, pale star,
but spiral on,
with motion your only
obligation.

Coyote Submits a List of Demands

I want the supremacy
of the auteur theory in film,
and of old men who'll sharpen
what has been dulled.

Repudiating the mithridatism
of television,
I long for black and red flags
over Tiananmen Square.

I demand that the ghost
of Robert Johnson
be installed as Speaker
of the House of Representatives,
and that "Love in Vain," "Spoonful,"
and "Terraplane Blues"
be granted favored-nation status.

Having seen the planets turn
and generations of mountains crumble,
I require the destruction
of climate-controlled
regional shopping multiplexes
and a precise account
of the jet stream's movement.

I yearn for continuity
from abacus to haruspex to zyxt,
and for absolute equality.

I insist on earning college credit
for expertise in ecotage.

Having lost all patience
with capitalism,
I demand sainthood for Villa
and the Flores Magón,
and the presence of gray wolves
on every corner.

I mandate frequent observations
of the anniversary of the Days of Rage,
and first-class postage stamps depicting
the head of Joaquín and Wounded Knee.

I announce an end
to Pyrrhic victories.
Amen.

Memorandum

FROM: Coyote
TO: William Casey

> To be sane in a mad world
> is bad for the brain . . .
>
> WENDELL BERRY

Lightning always strikes twice.

Don't protest with physics.
Too many knees
have been broken by your truncheons
to permit my genuflection
and silence on this point.

I confess this to you, o lord.
I confess.

Recorders are rolling
but I'll still write it in haze:
there is quite enough interpretation
and quite too much silence.

Flakes of bronze now ride my coat,
drifted down from the Dame de la Liberté.
Have them arrested.

You yearn, I know, for metempsychosis,
for transubstantiation, immortality.
But let me ask you this: since
the shadow government's been adumbrated,
who now casts the shadow?

For my part, I'll tell all.
I have allowed black widows
to build webs at the doors
and to wave their hourglasses
at passers-by.
I continue to honor Demeter,
and I have revealed state secrets
to the half-smiling girl
in the Dorian peplos.

In the country of the lambs, Director,
Coyote (*Canis latrans*) goes sleepless.

You have this all from other sources,
I know. But I'll howl it, o lord:
I confess.

Eamónn

When there was nothing else
we watched him working,
arms moving in tattered sleeves,
eyes burning in the desert sun,
staying low in the valleys
of a new land full of lightning.

Reattaching a Misplaced Head

In November of nineteen eighty-eight
Nathan Forrest's last army rose from the grave,
joined by a flock of pimply nazi punks
in this our kinder gentler America.
They marched singing in the culverts
and along suburban freeways
mostly—it pains me to say—unnoticed,
while opinionmakers lined the better streets
to watch a girl in a pop band squeak.

Meanwhile the nation had been sown with salt.
Federal agents produced clever instruments
to ferret out stores of fresh Alaskan water,
and scattered the limbs of vivisected chimps,
and combed such hair as the pit bulls shed
on our correctly distributed syllogisms,
while Thomas Jefferson himself,
with inspired resistance,
spat on Danforth Quayle's shoe.

That day I saw ten hundred thousand
hallucinations come to life,
some in good suits, some with cameras,
an assault rifle for every woman, man, and child,
and I was wide awake and rational.
Who could have peered ahead and guessed
that such ghosts would be reblooded
and given leave to roam the land?
Give up your surprise. This is only a start.

The Journey

for Rodney Peffer

One day the winds will blow cold,
Torrents of dust will be conjured up,
Whirlpools of leaves will block the way.

On that day we will turn
North to the mountains.
Rooms will be boarded shut,
Windows bolted.

Women will put on heavy clothing,
Children will free themselves of dreams,
Cloudshadows will stagger across the fields.

And we will lean against our broken fences
To wait for nights of endless snow,
Make plans to leave, but never go.

Punto Cabrillo

Rock and black water
Moonlight on sand
The dry land seeded
With water and rock

The candle burns on the table
Marking no time
The black water of the ocean rolls
Marking no time

The Revolution at the Zoo

Trained to bark, the seal sings
Falsetto near the closing time.
The penguin sprouts most comely wings.
The 'gator carpets over the slime.

Sing long and loud, call every way,
"Long live the revolution!"
The leopard casts a bust in clay.
The chimp perfects his elocution.

The Road to Cochise

The silence of these desert hills, in winter,
is deeper than the same silence
of these same hills, in autumn.

I have learned this in solitude,
having watched and listened carefully.

A deeper silence layers this wind.
But the same leaves dance
in the same snow, driven.

You talk for a moment, and then fall silent.
A colder wind rises. I begin to doubt.

Tapalpa

As the dew of Jalisco
slides over the green hills
	toward Salvador,
so the dew of Jalisco
hangs in clouds around islands,
obscuring the islands, low, wreathed,
and around the green hills
with their broken temples
that command a view
	toward Salvador:
So the dew of Jalisco
in its indifferent calm.

On a Metaphysician's Matchbook

One must study these matters:
The day was wet like a pane in Havana
or a gush of guava.
The night was wet, and wetter, too.
No simile would do.

And next dawn, dry flamingos
took wing for Guyana,
like the dry birds that had flown
to Guyana's dark glades
hour by hour the whole day before.

A Nightsong for Ed Abbey

Moab, Utah

The moon was a sliver of white when you died,
not even full.

But crows hovered furiously
in the air of wet fields,
doves kept watch in public places,
eagles wheeled over redwalled canyons,
and sirens limned the city's blackness,
torn at the edge by a tractor blade.

The planet turns and turns; it dances,
the only circle that will never break.
Warriors stand to defend its orbit,
subversive birds call and range through the shadows,
and the broken moon will not lull us again,
hearing the noisy night, awaiting your ghost.

Benediction

Again this year the war did not come.
But every night a black fog rises
from the unending highways of America,
and bombers hatch their crying brood
in the nests of fallen Salvador,
and Indians hug the grave's straight cut,
their blood like spots on an old man's hands.

No one ever asked such nights to fall.
Let us pray in their place for quieter hours,
the day's work done, by a brown desert river,
watching bats and lizards carve the darkness,
and birds shape cuttlefish bones into birds.

I am nearly young at this year's end.
But my nights are sleepless, infinite.
I lie awake in a dark room, waiting,
far from prayerful blood and swirling smoke,
watching the houses where others rest,
wishing them one more year of peace,
and sleep, sweet sleep until light of dawn.

Akhmatova, 1939

Was it you who dictated the pages of Hell
to Dante?

The old woman sits
tracing pictures in dust
on her writing table
with a shaking finger.

In the splintered sunlight
she hangs her head and weeps.
The years sting like horseflies.

The King of Andorra

If you found me drunk, wandering
through the Old Ghetto of Rome, or in some
diseased bodega on the outskirts of Sevilla,
I'd impress you with some sleight-of-hand,
a whispered confidence, a gestured command.

As it is, home and sober, I feel rather silly,
Decked out in ermine in a shoebox palace.
Well, look: I didn't ask for the job.

Maybe I'll stutter a bit of French
to reaffirm my sense of culture,
or lead an invasion of Liechtenstein,
in armor, on a charger,
or serve poisoned claret
to the Archbishop of Madrid.

Perhaps I'll discern
some plot against my throne:
    a crone in the plaza
    will tell all, panting,
    expecting a bounty
    or a diplomatic mission.

Perhaps I'll just take a sidestreet stroll,
recite a bit of doggerel,
jaywalk through a traffic circle,
terrorize a kittycat:
A king must be capable of anything.

Judge Crater

Did some conquering angel
come to lead you away, Judge Crater?
Or did you disappear, only
to resurface incognito
in sunny Acapulco?

If an alien starship descended
from the black Catskill night
to spirit you off to Andromeda,
let me know.
I'll be up in a flash.

If Ricky Ricardo
or the Fidelistas have you chained
to a conga drum, in some
humid canefield on the Cuban coast,
send a card.

I'll be searching high
and low for you, Judge Crater
(Amelia Earhart, too),
so wherever you be
keep that old eye peeled.

The Old Anarchists

Oam mashat', the yellow month,
and the old anarchists loll
beneath a greening mesquite,
arguing over the shapes of clouds,
having finished discussing mutual aid
and deconstructing the Internationale.
After hours and days of this
they have settled on the facts
of the death of God, some millennia ago,
and have shifted the conversation
to Lyov Bronstein, chained to a gun,
and one of them has produced a harp
and is playing a tune from Mississippi
about yellow months in Congo Square,
the nature of truth, the equinoxial precession,
human freedom, constant love,
and the thunderhead's form.

Alleys in Snow

A gray cat, or, in the proper light,
a black cat,
crouched quietly in the dominion
of an alley in Virginia,
as if he were mousing,
or preparing to mouse.

This is just as it was.
A gray cat sometimes black
does not admit of metaphor.
He is real and spectacular.
There was a black cat,
or a gray one.
It was winter.

And throughout that cold night,
the gray cat, not black now,
crouched in its corner,
waiting sphinxlike for mice.

In one house a man dozed off by the fire,
dreaming of solace and unending snow.
In another a woman
pushed scraps from her plate.

The black cat, unaware in the alley,
yowled.

A Portrait

This, too, is a Biblical landscape,
this desert with its mountains
like headstones. Here we learn
to affirm visions, to deny
all that we have ever become,
as Emil Nolde's harrowing knives
carved faces into blocks of oak,
reducing a man to a few quick strokes,
thin white slashes for eyes and mouth,
thinner incisions for the lines of age,
in the woodprint here above the desk,
among old books, to affirm what is left:
headstones, white slashes,
black strokes. Marks on paper.

Monument

In rotorwhipped air
the tracer's light:
sixty thousand sparks
lost to the night.

Death, the Killer Said

"Death," the killer said,
"always went with the territory.
I'll see you in Disneyland."
Thus writing his script
and animating it freehand
simultaneously,
cf. Wittgenstein—
for the killer in us all
says such clever things.

To the Fallen Republic

Be for me an assemblage of moments
and things that are beautiful:

the light of the moon on the Colorado,
the ponies that buck at Chincoteague,
the boatlamps at Pontchartrain,
near sunrise.

I am saddened by you as you are.
Be those.

Columbine at Soldier's Camp

A tangle of waters
amid arches of penstemon
and rhyolite cairns
a thousand years old.

I awoke in dawn's rose
surrounded by such things
and fell into the pages of Liddell and Scott
at the initial entry for *hamartia.*

The water glittered vainly.
A magpie called.
The day passed as any other.

Ma maidrín rua,
in the morning before sleep
you remembered Connemara
and said all this would endure,

but since we awoke in red morning
a language has died
somewhere in the shattered
skeleton of some forest.

The Last of the Free

Rexroth once remarked
that the times had changed
such that no one bothered anarchists.

Meaning, I take it,
that the age is so generalized
that each of us is the enemy.

It's not a condition to make one sane.
We turn up our collars, fearing the worst,
jumping at shadows, dour, defeated.
But rejoicing, the anarchic rain tumbles
down from the thirty-seven constellations
unhindered, and a mudspattered Apache
dances free through the pines of Cibecue.

On Reading That William Butler Yeats
Lies Forgotten in a Pauper's Grave

William Yeats is not at rest.
The hounds of Europe bay and howl
and scratch the stony ground of France,
tearing at dear William's bones
to drag him from eternity.

Unhonored guest, he lies among
the bludgeoned tramps of sweet Provence,
far from the imposter's mound
on Drumcliffe's wild and cheerless heights.
William Yeats is not at rest,
for Ireland has abandoned him,
let go her sleepless shanachie,
deprived him of her wet dark earth.

Cast a colder eye on this:
the nations fuel their endless hate,
we choke upon a thousand sins,
the songless world endures us still,
but William Yeats is not at rest.

Ceanannus Mór

I, another refugee, have forgotten
everything: the turns of the River Shannon,

the way the green land refuses its burdens
and sings itself in *dindsenchas*,

at night among towers, incantatory trees,
the constant rush of waves on the headland,

and cool lakes of still water
that once sheltered swans.

Schooled not in leechcraft but a sort of Latin,
and *béarla*, fine but unconvincing words,

I have come here to remember
what never was,

importuning these rivers and fields and islands
to surrender just one secret, to teach

a rare song of heroes, any of those things
our people centuries past unlearned,

having instead discovered history,
adrift, ignorant of what else to seek.

Versions

What is translation? On a platter
A poet's pale and glaring head,
A parrot's speech, a monkey's chatter,
And profanation of the dead.
VLADIMIR NABOKOV

Tripes *à la portuguese*

One day, in a restaurant, outside of space
and time,
they served love to me as a dish of cold tripes.
I called for the chef and said cautiously
that I would prefer them warm,
that tripes (and they were done *à la portuguese*)
were never eaten cold.

They grew impatient with me.
I couldn't be right—not in that place.
I didn't stalk out or change my order. I paid
and went outside to roam the streets.

Who knows what this means?
I don't know and it happened to me. . . .

I know that when we were children
we all had a garden,
ours, or public, or one of the neighbors'.
I know that then our only duty was play,
and that sadness is today's.

I know this all too well.
But if I ordered love, why did they bring me

Cold tripes cooked *à la portuguese?*
It's not a dish that can be eaten cold

And they brought it to me cold.
I didn't complain, but it was cold.
You can't eat it cold, but it came to me cold.

Written in a Book Abandoned on a Train

I'm coming in on the line from Beja.
I'm going in to the center of Lisbon.
I'm bringing nothing and I'll find nothing.
The expected fatigue of finding nothing,
My nostalgia's for neither past nor future.
I leave written in this book my epitaph:
I was grass and they didn't pull me up.

Gonzalo Rojas

The Turbine

Unicuique suum tribuere, to the fish
its fear, to this unfortunate
Sunday of flaming aluminum the clamor
of its perniciousness, to
these three or so hundred
Muslims in the spacious sky of Smyrna
their tall scimitar, their
noseless Allah;
            who
of these whoms, which
of these whiches will have sung among clouds?

Spasm

I write: the present of the poem is illusory.
Every mouthful measures, anticipates, calls,
    screams for relief;
Erases it, draws it like fatal farewells
    on railway platforms.
The nurse's needle explores the void, the vaulted
    emptiness my mind has made of my skin.
The woman's inhuman fingers perform.
The spasm dilates my organs—there's no room.
Every mouthful, monotonous as a wheel, begs
        for relief, demands it,
        transmits a mute, inconclusive dialog
        to the new hope, to the new goodbye.
There's no circle on Earth or living thing that flows
        in a single rush,
A single wave, a single sign. In the decay of the body
        that reveals its fragile
Wet and obstinate violence. Its ability
        to resist within the walls of a shell.

Four Black Poplars

As this line follows after itself
through the horizontal boundaries pursuing it
and, eternal fugitive, in the declining west
in which it seeks itself it dissipates
—as this same line
through its raised glance
turns all its letters
a diaphanous column
resolved as one untouched
unheard untasted but meditated
flower of vowels and consonants
—as this line that will not finish writing itself
and before devouring itself draws itself up
without ceasing to flow but always upward:
the four black poplars.

Aspiring
for the empty heights and there below
in the sky choked with water, duplicated,
the four are a single black poplar
and are none.

    Beyond, fronds in flames
that extinguish themselves—the evening adrift—
other black poplars now spectral tatters
undulate endlessly
endlessly immobile.
The yellow slips into rose,
the night twists itself into violet.

Between sky and water
—herbaceous calligraphy
traced over coals by the blowing wind—
is a blue and green fringe: earth.
It is one reflection hung within another.

Transitions: the winking eyes of the instant.
Each thing is its double, its phantasm;
the world disincorporates,
it is an apparition, it is four black poplars,
four violet melodies.
Fragile branches rise up from their trunks.
They are a bit of light and a bit of wind.
Immobile mooring-lines. With my eyes
I hear them murmur words of air.
Silence goes with the stream,
returns with the sky.

What I see is real:
four weightless black poplars
planted over a vortex.
A fixity that rushes
downward, upward,
toward the water of the sky of the pool
in a graceful toil that has no end
while the world lays anchor in darkness.
Pulse of final clarities:
fifteen minutes under a siege
that Claude Monet observes from a rowboat.

The sky is destroyed in the water,
the water negates itself in itself,
the black poplar is an explosion in violet:
the world is not solid.
Between being and non-being the grasses waver,
the elements soften,
the contours darken,
aspects, reflections, reverberations,
sparkling of forms and presences,
fog of images, occultations,
I see what we are: hallucinations.

Homero Aridjis

When Contepec Is Nothing More in the Night

When Contepec is nothing more in the night
than a stone
and the villages surrounding it
no more than names
the Altamirano plateau will be
the shadow of a wounded bird
in the golden dawn
crossing for a moment
the ever-present emptiness

This Black Stone

This black stone
Is a piece of night
That time has made palpable
So that a man
Can take up darkness in his hand

Labyrinth

Life a labyrinth, death a labyrinth,
Endless labyrinth, says the Master of Ho.

Everything enslaves, nothing sets free,
The suicide's reborn to some other suffering.

The prison opens onto another,
Each footstep drags another footstep.

Who thinks he can unroll
The roll, unrolls nothing.

Nothing flows anywhere. The centuries
Also live underground, says the Master of Ho.

Epitaph

Hiero's suckling nurse Silenis
liked her wine
nerve-numbing and often—
now she lies in this vineyard.
May her withered body
buried here among these grapes
refill in death the barrels
Silenis loved so well alive.

Hymn to Aphrodite

Leave Crete for this holy temple
Where a lovely grove of apple trees
Fringes an altar that smokes with incense
In your praise.

Shadows of roses fall on the ground,
And cold jets of water whisper in branches,
And shimmering leaves
Rain down deep sleep.

In the meadow stallions browse,
And wildflowers blossom,
And anise fills the air with fragrance.

Here, beloved Aphrodite, pour
Immortal nectar in golden cups,
Fill all with sudden ecstasy.

Endless Night

The moon has set,
and so too the Pleiades.
Midnight. Time passes.
I lie alone.

Obsession

When the heart is too full, the five senses
are impaired, the opposite of the statement
of Justine: "His heart has withered in him
and he has been left with the five senses,
like pieces of a broken wineglass."
LAWRENCE DURRELL, *Justine*

He is equal
    to the gods themselves,
I'd say:
That man who sits before you
    an inch away
and listens to your laughter,
your voice sweet with desire.

A hammerblow
falls on my heart.

When I see you
    the words
stand still on my lips,
my tongue stops.

A thin flame dances
like a maenad on my skin.

My eyes cloud over.
My ears ring with thunder.
The sweat pours. I tremble.
I am paler than salt-hay.

Panicked, I think
I'm about to die.

Alexandria: The Fall

We have tumbled into evil times;
We imagine this nightmare
    To be life itself.
Could it be that we've died
    And only dream that we live?
Or is it that we live
When life itself is gone?

Metapontum

The past is a world, and not a void of grey haze.
THOMAS CARLYLE

Troy: The First Day

A thousand vessels ride at anchor,
rimmed by the gray-eyed light of the stars.

I have counted them all,
know them all by their names,
by their colors and carvings,
the names of their captains.

I have numbered every flash of lightning,
flaring, crackling like seams of fat
on the masts and sails of a thousand ships.

I have remembered them all:
corsairs, planets, shields, faces,
harbors, fires on foreign coasts,
cities, the forgetful years ahead.
Seeing them, I know we have come too far.

Palinaurus

I slept in the curl
of a long green wave,
tumbling and turning.
The others went on.

From my bed offshore
I see the new cities,
the women, the fires,
the stone heads of the gods.

I lost in the contest.
But they won nothing.

Recent History

Once, I have heard, this land was just—
For a moment or two.
The rich turned it to dust.

after Martial VII, xciv

Economy

If you're born poor,
then get used to the grime.
Only the rich
get richer in our time.

after Martial V, lxxxi

The Fruits of Labor

Success, they say,
comes to those who work hard.
Look around. You'll see
that's a base canard.

after Martial V, iii

To a Critic

Only the dead enjoy your praise—
that's too expensive for my taste.

after Martial VIII, lxix

The Oligarch

Airplanes, yachts, and vaulting towers
bear the name of the new Diamond Jim.
The streets are awash in his dollars.
He'll not rest till the planet's named for him.

after Martial XII, x

Hellas

Out of cobble and ebbtide
a sea god arose,
and dribbled mosaics
upon the sand,

and left only a wine flask
and an old guitar
for you to strum
in the thundering night.

Ruins

The sacred groves
have been uprooted,
fenced in,
bought and sold,
sown with salt.
Listen to those
who clamor for fruit.

Ovid at Pontus

Men and women, particles,
lives shot through great accelerators,
not men and women in a civitas,
in a place where we can live.

It would be a fine thing to run,
to leave them all behind,
to slip into the sea,
forgetting whatever we knew of them,
and to arc past their cities,
to waste no more words,
to dive the ancient course of dolphins
gliding home to Metapontum.

The Gardens of Sallust

Alone in a strange country
with no small familiarities
except the chinking of glasses
and laughter from the street below,
in lyrical Italian, lovely tongue,

I think of Rimbaud,
running from the commonplace,
and of the quarrymen of Crete,
bowing their dark heads
to such a wild man as he,

And of the night
on a slim beach in Delaware,
a cold dark wind rising off the sea,
alone with *Le Bateau Ivre.*

Arthur Rimbaud, you know these streets,
the way the Corso d'Italia twists along
to embrace a hundred refugees
and diplomats, impeccably mannered.
With them, too, you wandered it drunk,
speaking an Italian as poor as mine,
nineteen merciless years old.

The wind turns its head
and stirs a little.
The summer that year was short,
you said.

A century later it burns long and wild
on its arc north from Egypt.
Someone's talk floats above the streets,
meager Italian caught in the plane trees.
The sirocco tears it away as it passes.

Lucania

The wind turns like a rose in the hand
over the broken fields,
the dry faces of plowmen,
a thousand brittle flowers.

The narrow tongue of that wind
licks the teeth of the earth,
the worn hands of farmers,
the soft bones of dead petals.

Jason at the Argo

I traveled far
to learn one truth:
all our lives we're victims
of the dreams of our youth.

Hekabe

The misery implicit
in the sound of the wind
is simply the sound
of a woman in tears.

The sound of the wind
is her voice, comminuting
the old walls
that case in this house.

Whispering now
through the empty rooms,
the terraces, the wind, her voice
rustles in the olive trees:

There is so little happiness
left in the world.

A Nativity

This much of the matter is known:
Osiris fathered a mortal son.
Howling dogs announced
his unexpected birth,
horses bucked, their riders cursed,
a comet streaked across the sky.
You can see it all before the dawn.

Kythera

Terrible Kythera, *Kythera deina,*
night storms the harbor:
the mask of light falls.

At night this island
is a spit of land,
crouching in darkness,
steam and foam, nameless.

At sunrise this island
will be Kythera again,
assuming the shapes
we allow it to know:

sea haze and dune grass,
saltwrack and promontory:
the terrible ceding to permanence.

In the Glass Mountains

The sun has fallen;
the mountains fill with shadow.
The spiraling stars
do not find you in their light.
I lie among them, alone.

Remember those stars,
how they bathed you in whiteness,
how they gathered you.
Now you flee from them, disdain
their embraces, and mine.

after Sappho

Callimachus at Pharos

A sea wind: the dune grass sighs.
Surf inscribes the estuary.
Cranes wing to Arabia.

I reach out my hand for another volume,
and black smoke rises.

Kalliope, beloved muse,
the shepherd sings to his flocks,
the water carrier to her spring.
But I have no more songs,
and I can make no more vows to ghosts.

A sea wind: the world crumbles at my touch,
pages of water, wind, and sand.

About the Author

Gregory McNamee's essays, short stories, poems, translations, and reviews have appeared in *The Bloomsbury Review, Exquisite Corpse, The Boston Review, The American Scholar, Parabola, The North Dakota Quarterly, Willow Springs,* and other journals in the United States and abroad. Many of his literary and political essays are collected in *The Return of Richard Nixon* (Harbinger House, 1990).

McNamee is coeditor, with James Hepworth, of *Resist Much, Obey Little: Some Notes on Edward Abbey* (Harbinger House, 1989), a collection of original essays by Barry Lopez, Wendell Berry, Diane Wakoski, and other writers. He is also editor of *Living in Words: Interviews from The Bloomsbury Review, 1981–1988* (Breitenbush Books, 1988). McNamee translated Sophokles's tragedy *Philoktetes* (Copper Canyon Press, 1987) from the Greek into English verse.

McNamee lives in Tucson, Arizona, where he works as an editor and writer.

Design by Ken Sánchez.

Text set in Trump Mediaeval by
G&S Typesetters, Inc., Austin, Texas.

Printed on acid-free paper and Smyth sewn
by Malloy Lithographing, Inc., Ann Arbor, Michigan.